PREDATOR VS PREY

Owl vs Mouse

Mary Meinking

www.raintreepublishers.co.uk
Visit our website to find out
more information about
Raintree books.

To order:

☎ Phone 0845 6044371

▤ Fax +44 (0) 1865 312263

▧ Email myorders@raintreepublishers.co.uk

Customers from outside the UK please telephone +44 1865 312262

Raintree is an imprint of Capstone Global Library Limited,
a company incorporated in England and Wales having its
registered office at 7 Pilgrim Street, London, EC4V 6LB
– Registered company number: 6695582

Edited by Rebecca Rissman, Dan Nunn,
    and Catherine Veitch
Designed by Joanna Hinton Malivoire
Levelling by Jeanne Clidas
Picture research by Hannah Taylor
Production by Victoria Fitzgerald
Originated by Capstone Global Library
Printed and bound in China by CTPS

ISBN 978 1 406 21866 4
14 13 12 11 10
10 9 8 7 6 5 4 3 2 1

British Library Cataloguing in Publication Data
Meinking, Mary.
Owl vs mouse. -- (Predator vs prey)
591.5'3-dc22
A full catalogue record for this book is available from the
British Library.

Acknowledgements
We would like to thank the following for permission
to reproduce photographs: Alamy Images pp. 10 (©
mammalpix), 20 (© Don Vail); FLPA pp. 5 (Gary K Smith),
15 (S Charlie Brown), 17 (Simon Litten), 19 (David
Hosking), 26 (Erica Olsen), 28 (Gary K Smith); istockphoto
pp. 6 (© S. Cooper Digital), 9 (© Jason Crader);
naturepl.com pp. 8 (Mike Read), 24 (Rolf Nussbaumer);
Photolibrary pp. 7 (Oxford Scientific/ Robin Redfern), 12
(age fotostock/ Dan Leffel), 18 (Oxford Scientific/ Tony
Tilford), 21 (Juniors Bildarchiv), 22 (Rolf Nussbaumer);
Photoshot pp. 4 (Woodfall), 13 (NHPA/ Ernie Janes), 14
(NHPA/ Stephen Dalton), 16 (NHPA/ Stephen Dalton), 23
(Imagebrokers), 25 (Imagebrokers), 29 (NHPA/ Jordi Bas
Casas); shutterstock pp. 11 (© Alexey Stiop), 27 (© Dr
Morley Read).

Cover photographs of a barn owl reproduced with
permission of Photolibrary (Peter Arnold Images/ Gerard
Lacz), and a field vole reproduced with permission of
Photolibrary (Oxford Scientific/ Mark Hamblin).

We would like to thank Michael Bright for his invaluable
help in the preparation of this book.

Every effort has been made to contact copyright holders
of material reproduced in this book. Any omissions will
be rectified in subsequent printings if notice is given to
the publisher.

Some words are shown in bold, **like this**. You can find
out what they mean by looking in the glossary.

Content

Talons vs tails

Claws scratch! Teeth gnaw! Two animals meet nose-to-beak in the grassy battlefield. Here's a silent hunter, the barn owl. It's up against a scampering challenger, the mouse.

mouse

owl

These animals live in fields across Europe. Other types of owls and mice live elsewhere. Both have strengths that will help them in this battle.

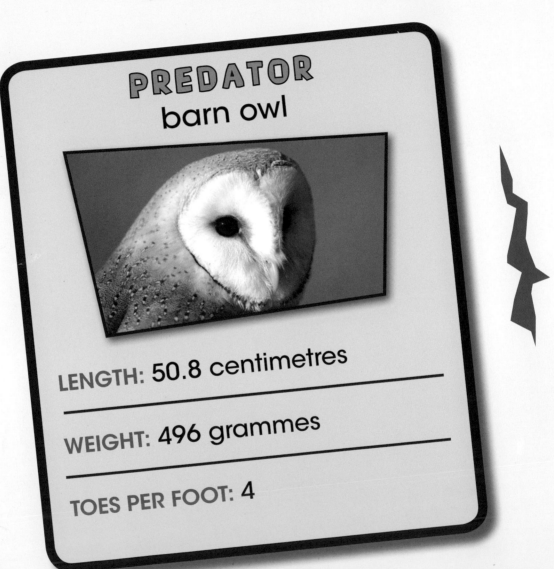

PREDATOR
barn owl

LENGTH: 50.8 centimetres

WEIGHT: 496 grammes

TOES PER FOOT: 4

Key
 where barn owls and mice live

PREY
mouse

LENGTH: 19.6 centimetres

WEIGHT: 56.7 grammes

TOES PER FOOT: 4 on front feet and 5 on back

Europe

Flying mouse trap

The barn owl is an excellent hunter. It uses its sharp claws, or **talons**, to catch and kill **prey**.

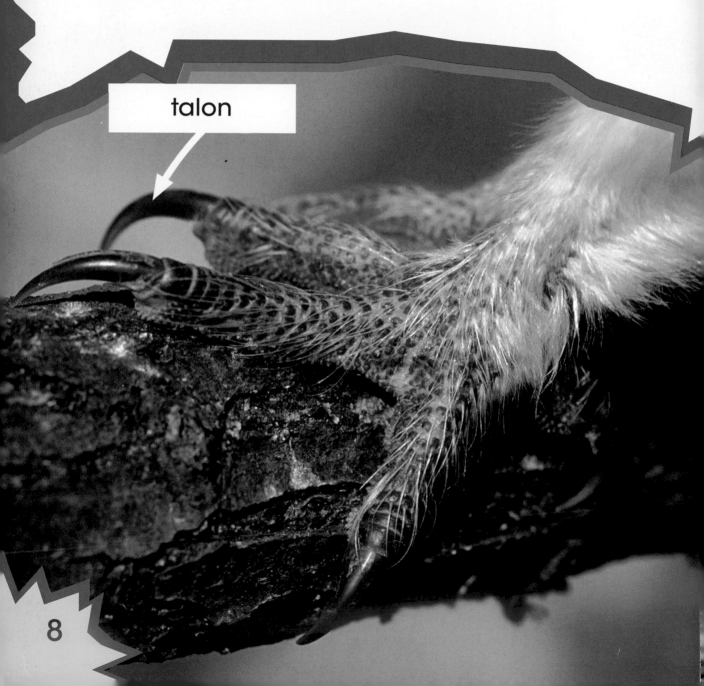

talon

DID YOU KNOW?

Barn owls' ears are hidden under their feathers. One ear is higher than the other. This helps the owl learn where a sound is coming from. They use their hearing to find prey in the dark.

Fast mice

If danger is near, the mouse darts under cover or back to its nest. It can run at 12 kilometres per hour. But can it run faster than an owl flies?

DID YOU KNOW?

Mice chew paths that are 2.5 to 5 centimetres wide through the grass. Mice use these hidden paths to move around without being seen.

Who's hungry?

The barn owl is a **carnivore**, or meat eater. It must eat one and a half times its weight in food every night. The mouse eats grass, plants, and tree bark. It eats over half its weight in food each day.

DID YOU KNOW?
The mouse stores some food underground to eat in the winter.

13

Night shift

At sunset, the mouse crawls out of its grassy nest. The owl wakes up from its nap. It climbs out of the tree hole where it hid all day. The owl hasn't eaten since last night. And it's hungry!

The mouse finds a seed to eat. It sits on its back legs and holds the food with its front paws. The owl sits on its **perch,** or resting place, listening for anything moving. It hears something. Is it a mouse?

DID YOU KNOW?
The owl's hearing is so good that it can hear a mouse under plants or snow.

The owl flies off its **perch**. It **glides** with its feet tucked back. It flies low and slowly towards the sound. It hears the animal hundreds of metres away.

DID YOU KNOW?

Owls' feathers have a fuzzy front edge. This **muffles,** or silences, the sound of their wings beating. This lets owls quietly sneak up on **prey**.

19

The mouse freezes. It sees something moving. The mouse stamps its hind foot, like a rabbit, to warn other mice. It runs towards its nest. The owl's wings open all the way out to slow down. Its tail feathers work like a brake to stop it.

DID YOU KNOW?

An owl's wings can be 85 centimetres across. That's as long as 8 mice in a line.

The owl's feet swing forwards with its sharp **talons** out. Even though it can't see the mouse, the owl hears it running. The owl snatches the running mouse with its talons.

mouse

The mouse tries to get free. It squeaks out a call for help. It wiggles and bites at the owl's feet. But it's trapped in the owl's strong **talons**. The owl grabs the mouse with its hooked beak. It takes off with its prize.

And the winner is...

...the owl! It returns to its **perch**. It gulps down the mouse, head first, without chewing.

DID YOU KNOW?

Owls swallow their food whole. The fur, bones, teeth, and feathers collect in their stomachs. There, it's made into balls called **pellets**. The owl soon coughs up and spits out the pellets.

pellet

What are the odds?

The barn owl catches nine out of every 10 animals it goes after. As well as mice it eats birds, rabbits, frogs, and other animals. It eats four to eight creatures every night. That's over 1,400 animals every year!

bird

Index